7 WOMEN THAT MADE LEMONADE WITH LIFE **LEMONS**

LEMONADE CHRONICLES

Book Anthology

Compiled by

Robin Johnson

Copyright 2022 by Robin Johnson

LEMONADE CHRONICLES
by Robin Johnson
All rights reserved. Printed in the United States of America. No part of this book may be used or produced in one's business, ministry or speeches without written permission, except for quotes or referring and giving credit to the author.

FIRST EDITION
Published by AB Enterprise LLC

ISBN: 97-98367613902

DISCLAIMER AND LIMITED LIABILITY:
Although many may find the tools, tips, strategies and/or teachings in this book helpful for their personal and professional growth and development, this book is sold with the understanding that neither the author nor AB Enterprise, LLC. is giving any specific financial, career, legal, psychological, emotional or spiritual advice. Nor is anything in this book intended to prescribe, cure or diagnosis any mental or emotional illnesses. If this book was purchased with that intent, please seek professional help. Every person's journey is different, which includes different outcomes and different solutions. This book promises no outcome for any situations and it should be used for coaching purposes only. This book does not replace professional help, and although the author is a professional in coaching, she does not write with the intent to cure, diagnose or prescribe any mental or emotional diseases. You may reach out to Coach Robin or other authors for additional help in one on one coaching.

This book cannot be reproduced or copied by anyone else other than the creator and author.

Table of Contents

Chronicle 1
Apostle Robin Johnson
It's Bitter Sweet………………………………………………………… **05**

Chronicle 2
Apostle Yvette Levell
Beautifully Broken…………………………………………………… **16**

Chronicle 3
Shequana Dorin
From Being Rejected to Always Accepted…………………… **29**

Chronicle 4
Siza Chaplin
Bodly Bald……………………………………………………………… **39**

Chronicle 5
Shonte Youmans
Get Out………………………………………………………………… **49**

Chronicle 6
Lady S
Unrighteous Judgment…………………………………………… **58**

Chronicle 7
Michelle Cofer
Never Bitter, Always Better……………………………………… **69**

Introduction

As a leading lady who's endured many sour patch moments, and yet with God, I overcame them all. Who would think, as a young girl, I loved "sour patch," candy almost thrown in the towel when real life threw her some sour blows? But, when I realized I could peel, cut, boil, and a little sugar, what was sour became a life-saving pitcher of greatness. As the visionary of this great project, I overcame sexual betrayal, verbal abuse, abandonment, divorce, and character assassination none destroyed me.

This anthology is full of real-life stories, like mine, about women who deliberately decided not to be bitter but better. To view their sour patch moments as an opportunity to peel, cut, boil, and a little sugar, what was sour became a life-saving pitcher of greatness. I sincerely hope you get inspiration, encouragement, and unction to turn life's lemons into lemonade.

-Robin

Chronicle 1

It's Bitter Sweet

Apostle Robin Johnson

> *"28 And we know that in all things God works for the good of those who love him, who[i] have been called according to his purpose. 29 For those God foreknew he also predestined to be conformed to the image of his Son, that he might be the firstborn among many brothers and sisters. 30 And those he predestined, he also called; those he called, he also justified; those he justified, he also glorified."*
>
> *Romans 8:28-30 NIV*

𝓑eing a LEADING lady can often feel BITTER & Sweet. Yet, with the day-to-day discovery, you realize it doesn't matter how charismatic, pretty, and fashionable you are; development evolves through each bitter-sweet moment.

"As a girl with great imagination, seer, and unheard-of dreams, you will face many who desire to strip your coat. The Horror of demonic encounters, traps, empty promises, pitfalls, and mental imprisonments, however, you will be triumphant and sit with many Kings." -Robin. This a true statement in introspection of life path.

With each bitter moment, the immediate perception is defeat. What an outlier, life lemons challenge you to make lemonade. Lemons are bitter; when used in the right environment or combination, they can be sweet. According to Webster's dictionary, the lemon is a fruit with many beneficial factors. Ironic life renders bitter setbacks. Like the lemon, each bitter blow produces practical elements. Produce, manufacture from components; ever bitter setback manufactures advantageous components to produce greatness.

The yellow, odd-shaped oval bitter citrus fruit **stimulates** heart health, **helps** control weight, **prevents** kidney stones, **protects** against anemia, **reduces** cancer risk, and **improves** digestive health. Proof that every odd-shaped circumstance and bitter setback is the canvas for discovery and elevation.

Stimulation is surviving a mentally abusive marriage laced with many traumatic sexual betrayals. "Rumors of pregnancy, hotel shenanigans, bewitchery transgression with women; one betrayal stab after another induced inner hemorrhage."

-Robin

Instigation provoked me to create lucrative women's enrichment workshops. A bitter setback is a synergetic way to stimulate and facilitate the motivation to develop or increase activity in (a state or process).

Help, through the valley of divorce, this bitter setback constructed a space for self-discovery. "Hear me; self-discovery saved my life; it blossomed determination with independent strength; I triaged, assessed, and mended my wounds." -Robin.

Bitter setbacks succor as a life preserver, allowing the essence of self-awareness.

Prevent, brief homelessness, abandonment, mental abuse, and tremendous scandals were bitter setbacks; however, they averted me from self-sabotage. Without the trauma, I would've never accomplished elevation in the Lord's church. Prevention of undermining my power and authority to achieve greatness.

Protect, a qualified safeguard, successful Entrepreneur, philanthropist, motivational speaker, and more; bitter setbacks activated compassion for the degraded and underdog. As a preserver and defender, I've co-founded multiple Ministries and participated in several established non-profit organizational boards, each focusing on the issues of the lost and forsaken.

Reduce, discovered self fragrance, sweet attributes striving through bitter setbacks which decreased inadequate feelings and triggers—constructing an environment for creativity, healing. Reduction rids the toxic while thickening and concentrating qualities.

Improve, life sweeten "my heart finally smiles as I embrace the totality of femme, gal, matron, me. Girl, embracing every imperfection, stretch mark, long wavy hair, and big hips!" - Robin

Bitter setbacks surprisingly enhance value and quality of life. They have amplified each essential unique faction thrusting into satisfaction.

Like a lemon, under pressure, you've discovered versatility. Lemon usage is from culinary to medicinal. The lemon distracted oil usage range from healing, stain remover, a fragrance for perfumes, soaps, skin creams, and an antibacterial compound that cure mouth infections like gingivitis.

Bitter Sweet conditions produce the ability to adapt to many different functions or activities. Therefore, your function is more significant than perceived. "Lemonade Chronicles Anthology" is full of leading ladies who've adapted-make (something) suitable for a new use, purpose, or modify.

Leading ladies that transformed yield development and evolution through every **bittersweet season.**

"Joseph had a dream, and when he told it to his brothers, and they hated him even more. He said to them, "Listen to this dream I had: We were binding sheaves of grain out in the field when suddenly my sheaf rose and stood upright, while your sheaves gathered around mine and bowed down to it." *Gen 37:5-7 NIV*

"...So, Joseph went after his brothers and found them near Dothan. But they saw him in the distance, and before he reached them, they plotted to kill him. "Here comes that dreamer!" they said to each other. "Come now, let's kill him and throw him into one of these cisterns/pits and say that a ferocious animal devoured him. Then we'll see what comes of his dreams." and they took him and threw him into the cistern. The cistern was empty; there was no water in it." *Gen 37:17-24 NIV*

" So, Pharaoh sent for Joseph, and he was quickly brought from the dungeon. When he had shaved and changed his clothes, he came before Pharaoh. Pharaoh said to Joseph, "I had a dream, and no one can interpret it. But I have heard it said of you that when you hear a dream you can interpret it." "I cannot do it," Joseph replied to Pharaoh, "but God will give Pharaoh the answer he desires." *Gen 41:9-16 NIV*

Just like Joseph, these leading ladies' evolved through every **bittersweet season.**

Bitter Sweet Perspective

With each bitter moment, the immediate perception is defeat. What an outlier, every bitter setback simulates beneficial components of exponential self-growth.

1. Commence your heart-

"Keep vigilant watch over your heart; that's where life starts."

Proverbs 4:23 MSGV

2. Remove distractions-

"Keep your eyes straight ahead; ignore all sideshow distractions." Proverbs 4:25 MSGV

3. Convert your perspective-

"And be not conformed to this world: but be ye transformed by the renewing of your mind, that

ye may prove what is that good, and acceptable, and perfect, will of God." Romans 12:2 MSGV

-Robin

How has the chapter simulated your perspective on every bitter setback as a beneficial component for exponential self-growth?

_____

_____

_____

_____

Apostle Robin Johnson

I'm a mother of four and a grandmother. I cherish family; it's my first ministry/passion. My second passion unmistakably is serving people, singing gospel music, and delivering the gospel. I've co-founded multiple Ministries and participated in several established non-profit organizational boards, each focusing on the issues of the lost and forsaken. An asset to countless churches, children, youth, and women ministries,

I've served as a Praise and Worship Leader, Youth empowerment Leader, Teacher, Prophetess, Minister, and Elder. On Aug 31, 2012, a significant milestone was the installation to serve Created with Promise and Potential Ministries as a Pastor in Hampton, GA. Later renamed Created To Win, the central hub housed in Charlotte, NC, was established in 2019.

The Overseer of C2W Ministries International establishing hubs in Ghana within the Tema & Accra regions! Affectionately, known by many for women's enrichment and sisterhood, is at the top of my list; I birthed Woman to Woman Impartation (WTWI) ministry and annual WTWI conferences in 2012. In addition, I birthed Side Piece No More (SPNM)

Enrichment Workshop in 2017 after surviving a mentally abusive marriage laced with many traumatic sexual betrayals. In 2021, the Apostolic elevation marked a humbling achievement.

I have a multifaceted, diverse background; administration, management, finance, workshop facilitator, symposium architect, organizational development ingenuity, event planning, marketing strategist, radio hostess, best-selling author, motivational speaker, and entrepreneur. I sincerely believe my eyes have not seen nor my ears have heard; what YAH (God) has yet to reveal concerning my life.

Connect via

Email: pastorrldodson@gmail.com
Instagram: @pastorrobinministries
Facebook: @pastorljohnson
Tel: (980) 349-6140

Chronicle 2

Beautifully Broken

Apostle Yvette Levell

"My sacrifice, O God, is a broken spirit, a broken and contrite heart". Psalms 51:17 KJV

"When you pass through the waters, I will be with you, and when you pass through the rivers, they will not sweep over you, when you walk through the fire you will not be burned, the flames will not set you ablaze". Isaiah 43:2 KJV

What does it mean to be broken or to experience brokenness? Webster's dictionary defines brokenness (to be broken) as forcibly separated into pieces, to be torn apart, to be violated, to be incomplete. Brokenness is a place of total transformation. Going through the process is not comfortable or beautiful in any way, shape, or form. Yet, that journey to beauty is where your faith in God and who He has made you be becomes illuminated.

We sometimes need help understanding our brokenness. We don't want to or can't see "beauty" in it. But if we relinquish our hurts and brokenness to Him, we will experience the beauty. Finding beauty in brokenness comes from confidence in God and how He works in our lives. It's trusting in Him to repair and restore us. We find beauty in brokenness when we sit with Him and pour out all our pain and struggles, knowing He is listening to each word. Ultimately, we'll feel His peace when we stand in His promise.

Beauty is Not so easily Seen~

One day I was sitting waiting at a doctor's appointment. As I scanned the room, I saw a painting that looked very interesting to me. When I inquired about the name of it and the concept, the receptionist stated the name of the picture was entitled "Consider the Lilies" by Makoto Fujimura. Little did I know that hiding in the background of the painting, not seen at first glance, was a "lily". So I Googled the artist, and his description of the picture caught my attention.

This painting was painted using more than 80 layers of finely crushed minerals in a Japanese art style known as "Nihorga," a style Fujimura called: "slow art" Looking closely, it reveals layers and layers of complexity and beauty. Look at your life and how we can have so many complex things we've experienced, but at first glance, the true beauty is not so evident. Fujmara technique echoes the making "beauty through brokenness," it depicts how life has many layers hidden behind the beauty of God and who He made us to be.

We become God's masterpiece. When we think of a masterpiece, we think of perfection. The definition of a masterpiece is a work of outstanding artistry, skill, or workmanship, just like in the painting mentioned earlier. Ephesians 2:10 says we are God's workmanship. We are a piece of our master, our GOD.

You may ask how something broken has beauty. I'm glad you asked; broken things are usually tossed away, discarded, and considered "useless". Unfortunately, people can feel useless and tossed away too. I've been there, and it's not a good place to be in at all. I have experienced various types of "Brokenness," So, let's define brokenness; what does it mean? Brokenness can take many shapes and forms, such as unemployment, illness, addictions, ending of relationships, divorce, and even death. All of these can lead to feelings of exhaustion, loneliness, anger, and fear.

I've learned that none of us get through life without trials and painful life circumstances; multiple can appear out of nowhere, and very painful, feeling like you're in a nightmare. Growing up, I've personally experienced a life of rejection, and resentment, to name of few. I experienced rejection from the womb, not wanted by either parent (God predestined me) even if my mother and father weren't ready.

Many days brought heartache, wondering where my next meal would come from, maturing beyond my age to support my mother, raising me and my siblings by herself.

Broken emotionally (no connection with my mother, only my grandmother), mentally broken (felt crazy), and financially ruined (living in poverty); what helped us was our Faith in God that was not "broken". So many days, I wished for a new life that would bring me hope that hadn't come.

The Lord is Near to the Brokenhearted~

There is One who seeks out and loves the broken and rejected. God is looking for the broken ones who need healing, comfort, and restoration. He is a healer, an artist who picks them up, sees their brokenness, and turns them into beautiful masterpieces. Who is it, you may ask? It's JESUS.

God uses Broken People~

Hannah felt broken by her infertility; that was my story. I was married for two years, and my husband and I tried to conceive once we did, I had four miscarriages. A broken woman who longed to give birth and become a mother. I felt like I wasn't a "whole woman". The following year the Lord blessed me to adopt twins who are now 29 years old. There are other examples, such as Moses being a murderer and being in exile. Joseph's brothers abused him and sold him into slavery. Mary Magdalene suffered horribly from demonic possession. And Peter denied Jesus three times, then ran away in shame, guilt, and fear. If you read every story of brokenness in the Bible, you'll see God using broken, hurting people to bring hope into the world. He holds them close and heals their hurts. He comforts, rebuilds, and restores their lives. Joseph told his brothers, "You intended to harm me, but God intended it for god to accomplish what is now being done, the saving of many lives." Genesis 50:20 NIV

How does God use Broken Things~

Rest Assured, God will use your brokenness as a tool for his glory. There is a skill called Kintsugi if this is the first time you have heard of it. Kintsugi and brokenness relate to how God takes the brokenness of our lives and makes something beautiful. Kintsugi is the Japanese word translated as "golden" joinery" or "golden repair." When Japanese pottery was broken, it was never thrown away. Instead, the pottery was gathered and mended again by mixing lacquer and powdered gold. So instead of throwing away the seemingly useless dish, the container's brokenness remains part of the dish's history. Even when we look back on our past and the things that us, it is our testimony.

I looked for methods to mend my broken heart through drugs, alcohol, and living a promiscuous lifestyle. God takes all my broken piece (I am the clay; he is the potter) to make me beautiful. He uses our hurt to help us lean on His strength to encounter Him in ways we never have. Jesus never sees us broken beyond repair. Our brokenness can bring us the power we didn't know we were capable of and help us be an inspiration to others.

God's power will use your brokenness of spirit while walking the broken way. Not only that, God isn't going to hastily spackle up the cracks in us with temporary solutions that will fail in the future. Just like the kintsugi, your brokenness will be filled with GOLD and the hope of the glory of God. God will NEVER waste your brokenness; there is beauty in it.

How did I Realize I was Beautifully Broken~

I became like the woman with the alabaster jar as I opened it before my savior. I cried out to him in my sadness. I embraced the brokenness, and where it came from so, I could lay it at the feet of Jesus. I position myself as the woman did by kneeling as the tears hit his feet. The beauty of the pain now began to heal me, so my sadness turned to joy.

God will use your Brokenness for Growth in Christ~

Brokenness can yield beautiful fruit as our will is crushed, molded, and made to the Will of God. The only place we should turn to our brokenness is to the Lord. You risk becoming bitter towards the Lord when you hold your heartache. Brokenness results in humility, contrite and genuine healing. As I lay my brokenness down at the feet of Jesus, he healed me; the beauty of who He made me be is the greater purpose for my life.

Beauty in Brokenness is Necessary~

Lastly, there are plenty of times that I look back and ask God why those things had to occur in my life. As much as it broke me, I could hear a whisper tell me, "my brokenness produced pure worship in total surrender." TO GOD BE THE GLORY FOR THE THINGS HE HAS DONE.

Beautiful Perspective

Bitter setbacks surprisingly enhance value and quality of life. Your brokenness was not to kill you but gain a beautiful perspective on how essential it is to:

1. Smile and always pray-

"Always be joyful. Never stop praying. Whatever happens, give thanks, because it is God's will in Christ Jesus that you do this." 1 Thessalonians 5:16-18 GWV

2. Stand firm-

"He will be like a tree that is planted by water. It will send its roots down to a stream. It will not be afraid in the heat of summer. Its leaves will turn green. It will not be anxious during droughts. It will not stop producing fruit." Jeremiah 17:8 GWV

-Robin

How has the chapter provided clarity and perspective on your times of "brokenness"?

_____

_____

_____

_____

_____

_____

_____

Apostle Yvette N. Levell

I was born in Newark, NJ, on June 25, 1967. In 2001 I was installed as the Pastor of Everlasting Covenant Ministries in East Orange, NJ, until 2012, when the ministry relocated to Southern NJ. In 2017 the ministry name was changed and relaunched as Living PROOF Ministries, Inc until 2019. At the end of 2019, the Holy Spirit impressed upon my husband and me to hold fellowship services bi-monthly in Newark, NJ, at Living Logos Christian Assembly. Therefore, in 2021 I became a part of the ministerial staff at Living Logos Christian Assembly until 2022.

I work diligently with my husband of 31 years, Apostle Eugene Levell, in many facets of ministry. I'm the mother of adult twins Kion (daughter-in-law Patricia) and daughter Kiona and grandmother of 3 granddaughters, Ky'rah, Ceani', and Sy'rae. I'm the founder and C.E.O. of Heart of Love Outreach Ministries Inc (H.O.L.). H.O.L. is a ministry focused on counseling and ministering to those living with HIV/AIDS; I'm the founder of Matter's of the heart wellness Ministries and Iron Sharpens Iron L.L.C./Training Center and Lead Intercessor of Living Proof Ministries Prayer Network.

God called me to the ministry of reconciliation, healing, and exhortation. I'm committed to healing the whole man: mind, body, and spirit. My ministry focus is both single and married women, as God has empowered her to effectively deal with the hurts and issues they face daily. I serve as a vehicle through which Christ brings complete deliverance and healing. I function in many facets of ministries such as Sunday School, Bible Study teacher, Praise and worship Leader, Pastor, and now Apostle in the Lord's church.

Educationally I've achieved certificates in General Bible, Evangelism, and teacher's training at Eastern Bible Institute in Newark, NJ. She has received her certification as a Christian Counselor at the Lighthouse International Ministries. I have a diploma in Addiction counseling from ICDC College, Associate Degree in Health and Human Sciences at Ultimate Medical Academy, and a Certified Professional Life Coach at Transformation Academy. NACC Certified Christian Counselor, NACC Grief, and Loss Counselor. Presently enrolled in the dual degree (Bachelor/Master) program at Christian Bible Institute, graduating September 2023. Lastly, I am the author of my first book, "Not yet...Live to testify and Co-author of The Lemonade Chronicles Anthology 2022.

As a true worshipper, my heart follows hard after God. I reach out to those in need with love and compassion by faith, believing I can help individuals meet and take hold of their God-given destiny. Most importantly, I love the Lord with my whole heart, soul, and mind.

Chronicle 3

From Being Rejected to Knowing that I'm always Accepted

Shequana Dorin

"I praise you because I am fearfully and wonderfully made; your works are wonderful, I know that full well."
Psalms 139:14 NIV

As my hand began to write my story, I asked that the reader open up her heart, eyes, and ears and see God's hands move. Pages that explain how a rejected person responds, starting from birth until they receive Jesus. Once you push toward Jesus, everything about your life changes, knowing and accepting that it doesn't matter who rejects you; the Lord God gets who you are.

On July 1, 1986, a little girl was born in a small town called Byron, Georgia; fantastic parents Kathy Jackson and Sammie Lee Price. On August 31, 1987, a traumatic accident occurred, and as a result, Shequana was placed in the arms of Dora Elizabeth Christopher and Sampson Smith, Sr., now raised in their home, brought about a change in many ways. Growing up, she was confused, rejected, and never felt she belonged. She often heard people talk negatively about her mother and father but never understood why. Then, shockingly, Shequana realized Dora wasn't her mother and arranged to meet her biological parents.

Sadly, beginning of an identity crisis, parental rejection instituted abandonment to take root. At an early age, questions would arise, who am I? Feelings of emptiness, void, and darkness loomed over me. My life had no structure; I lay awake in bed with suicidal thoughts. "Oh my God, I will kill myself," crying many nights.

Challenged and often bullied in school, children haunt that my mother was a prostitute. The children whispered that my father was a married man and won't acknowledge my existence. Crying, I'll ask, "Why are people saying these horrible things about my family? Are these things true?" inquired repeatedly. Then, finally, the reply, "Yes, but don't worry about what the kids say. They are not your mom and Dad. We are."

Life continued, feeling cold, confused, and dark without hope. Questions of identity created a shaky foundation that began to crumble. I began to hold on tight to whomever or whatever she could find. At 18, I gave birth to my firstborn son. He brought temporary joy; unfortunately, the delivery did not fix me. Instead, it exposed my issue of finding love, acceptance, and feeling complete. As a result, I commenced living in a place of hurt. Continuously in pursuit of love in all the wrong places. Drifting from relationship to relationship and town-to-town until she ended up in a pit called "hell." The pit consisted of living an empty life in a dark hole of drugs, jail, prostituting, lying, loneliness, homelessness, and barely existing.

    Then, one day a man entered my path and thought, "this is the answer key to every problem." As a walker of dark places, I felt undeserving of light for years. Then, finally, this man seemed to bring light while being a provider; we gave birth to a baby girl. But, unfortunately, quickly finding the answer key was outside a man.

    In seeking acceptance, I rekindled my relationship with my former boyfriend. Home from prison, he abandoned me for another man. Again, I'm devastated another man rejected me. What does another man have that I don't have? Crying out to God, I asked Him why is my life filled with pain, hurt, and anger. At this point, God began to wipe tears away. God comforted was holding me in His loving arms. Breakthrough, I began to see God move in my life. I attended college and graduated as an EMT – Emergency Medical Technician. Just as she thought life was going great. I forgave my former boyfriend and lived together; things were beautiful at first. We started using drugs and became pregnant; he exited my life for a man. I wanted to commit suicide by smoking meth, desperately trying to kill my unborn daughter and myself. I had a nervous breakdown; doctors initiated the

Family and Children Services, taking my newborn and children.

A significant turning point was that I began to live and accomplish many dreams and goals through prayer. God began to speak and showed my shame, guilt, and mistakes. I screamed, "I FORGIVE ME!!" I dusted and picked myself up and let everything go! God's unconditional love spoke to my heart. In God's bosom, there's peace, acceptance, and the love I was longing for. What I craved starts with loving and respecting myself. I gave myself permission to heal and obtain true agape love.

Now, Queen God created me to love, live, and laugh. God restored, repaired, and corrected relationships destroyed. I celebrate myself as Minister Shequana Williams Dorin. I moved forward, allowing God to "JUMPSTART," the Queen that was inside. The enemy wanted me dead, but God has given me life more abundantly. Accepting the love is easy, from my husband and our four beautiful kids. The secret key to being accepted is to accept God's love, ways, and will for your life. My story started in despair and pain; today, God has blessed me with a new life. A mentor told me, "It's time to take flight; get off the tarp"-Pastor Robin.

As a mother, wife, college graduate, and ordained minister. Who is living my best life. No more being rejected, but I know I'm always accepted because of God.

Knowing Your Accepted Perspective

Like a lemon, under pressure, you'll discover the versatility within. So instead of focusing on rejection, acknowledge your acceptance.

1. Ways to acknowledge your accomplishments:

- Throw yourself a party.
- Treat yourself to something special.

2. Allow, give permission to, or for; permit yourself:

To cry, fail, and make mistakes in your journey of discovering yourself as "accepted."

-Robin

How has the chapter stimulated your focus on how you are "accepted"?

_____

_____

_____

_____

_____

_____

_____

_____

Shequana Dorin

I was born in 1986 in a small town in Warner Robins, Georgia. I'm the fourth child out of five total siblings; months after being born, I almost drowned and was placed in foster care custody, awarded to Dora Christopher. I attended a local public school and graduated from Youth Challenge Academy High School. Growing up in church, I faithfully sang in the youth choir and participated in vocation bible school at a young age. I recognized and nurtured the anointing and calling on my life.

I've served in various capacities of leadership throughout the years. In 2015 I founded "Jumpstart Queen's," an organization empowering Hurting women as Godly queens of purpose and destiny. I have a medical office Specialist Diploma from Middle Georgia Technical College. In 2013 I graduated from Central Georgia technical college as a licensed Emergency Medical Technician. Also, in 2020 I graduated from Beulah Heights University with an Associate degree in Religious Studies. My husband, Mark Dorin, and our children, Zay, Alaina, Aria, and Anthony Dorin, supported me. When all is said and done, I want to see people fully embrace

God's love and walk in victory and power while experiencing the fullness of God's promises.

Chronicle 4

Boldly Bald

Siza Chaplin

> *"Now a woman, having a blood flow for twelve years, who spent all her livelihood on physicians and could not be healed by any, came from behind and touched the border of His garment. And immediately her flow of blood stopped."*
>
> Luke 8:43-44 KJV

From a very young age, we are taught to turn lemons into lemonade literally. When we did not have any juice to drink as children, my grandmother used to say – go and pick some lemons outside so you can make lemonade. We excitedly did that because we enjoyed the adventure of climbing the trees, which we were mainly forbidden to do without adult consent.

All my cousins would grab their fresh lemon, slice it up to squeeze the juice out, and add cold water and lots of sugar. That's when my sweet tooth started. We enjoyed it thoroughly but not realizing the lessons that came with that drink. My grandmother always quoted this statement when I would complain to her about something that happened to me at school "When life gives you lemons, make lemonade." So when I finally understood its meaning, I trusted and believed that I would look for a way to turn it into something sweet in every situation that turned bitter.

No different when it came to My hair loss journey. I started losing my hair in my prime years. Usually say that because I had just turned 30 when I found my first bald patch – the size of a quarter on the right side of my head, tucked behind my ear. When I woke up the next day, there was a giant smooth bald patch on the crown of my head.

These two incidents shocked me but also left me confused. What was happening to me, and who shaved my hair in my sleep? It couldn't have been anyone because I lived by myself. Was I getting cancer? Don't judge me; most people thought its only people with cancer that lost their hair, so I assumed the same. After day 2 of finding that bald spot, I became anxious about when to find the next one and the next one.

My anxiety became my reality because I would find a new bald spot every week, then it was every other day until it became daily. I started panicking and consulted physicians – four to be exact, and they all gave me the wrong diagnosis. I felt like the woman with the issue of blood in the bible Luke 18. If it wasn't due to stress, it was hormones or braiding.

Finally, they gave me an answer, but it didn't make anything better because there was no solution. My hair kept falling out.

Since the doctors couldn't give me a solution, I was determined to find my answer. So I started researching on Dr. Google and took the advice of anyone who cared to share home remedies that cure hair loss. I tried almost everything, from washing my hair in horse shampoo to massaging my scalp with essential oils, coconut oil, onion juice, or any other concoction I would come across. Phew, the smell was sometimes unbearable, but I had to do what I had to do.

At this point, I had already lost a considerable amount of hair, and any solution gave me hope. Unfortunately, until I realized the condition was worsening, I didn't have a proper diagnosis. Finally, I'm issued a referral to a highly recommended and experienced dermatologist. Unfortunately, getting an appointment with her took another three months, and during that time of waiting, I always looked for alternative help.

Hurdling my mental health, I became depressed and had suicidal thoughts repeatedly. It knocked down my self-esteem, and I hated the person who stared back at me in the mirror. I was losing my hair rapidly, and my skin was also changing. My face, neck, and arms were becoming discolored. I now know it was hyper pigmentation. My eyebrows had chipped away as well as my eyelashes were disappearing. I felt like I was becoming an alien on earth.

This process was the most challenging time in my life, but I've realized that we can transform any painful situation into opportunities for growth and learning. Life can sometimes be unbelievably beautiful, with everything coming together to create a moment of pure, unadulterated bliss. For example, I grew up with a beautiful head full of hair and was playing around with my hair by trying out different hairstyles that were trending at that time.

Life can also be awful, with situations being incredibly unfair and heartbreaking, like losing my hair at the most crucial time in my life of looking to settle down and be someone's wife. This harrowing experience would have resulted in me allowing the circumstances to throw a non-ending pity party. Losing my hair by force led me down a very dark period of depression that lasted a couple of years and could've ended my life.

I'm grateful I rose from the ashes like a phoenix and didn't allow myself to be a victim forever. I mourned the loss of my hair for many years and finally came to accept that what I couldn't change, I had to accept. I survived self-pity, suicide, and low self-esteem.

Now I know that the difference between a victim and a survivor is the ability to take the crappiest moments in life and turn them into fertilizer. When we can use these painful times as fuel for our personal growth, we can move through any difficulty with grace and resilience. My hair loss journey has been the most arduous growth I had to endure but in 1 Corinthians 10:13, God promised us that He would never give us anything we can't bear. Each season in our lives is here to help us write a different part of our story.

I finally got my diagnosis a year later. It was alopecia areata, which occurs when the immune system mistakenly attacks the hair follicles for reasons that are not clear and causes hair loss. A diagnosis makes it better because it gives closure and answers to the questions you keep asking yourself while you are still going through all the symptoms. It helps you to get to the root of the problem and find a solution.

Unfortunately, in my case - alopecia has no cure. It is an autoimmune condition that is not life threatening and does not cause physical pain. However, the psychosocial effects of hair loss can be devastating.
As of writing this chapter, I have lost 90% of my hair and I am permanently bald because I now have scarring alopecia coupled with the complete loss of my eyebrows. Thankfully, I have micro-bladed my eyebrows with semi-permanent brows. So I wake up with eyebrows on fleet.

I now live my life boldly, bald and proud. I have become a global alopecia ambassador who advocates for awareness worldwide. I have a free private support group on Facebook called 'Global Alopecia Movement,' whose mandate is to empower women living with hair loss to regain their confidence, boost their self-esteem, and help them with coping strategies. In addition, the movement aims to empower 'alopecia warriors' to own their bald or patchy 'crowns' in a superficial world that judges beauty by what grows on your scalp.

I also published a book titled "Enough Already!" Overcoming the stigmas of alopecia is available on Amazon. This book was my coming out of the 'closet' project. It helped me announce to the world that I was living with alopecia, but it was also a tool I used to help other women who were losing their hair and couldn't understand why and what was causing it. It is a reference point for many, even today, on managing the condition. My hair loss journey led to my international public speaking career taking off and helping to inspire millions of people around the globe, which happens to be my passion.

Bold Perspective

Like the lemon, each bitter blow produces

practical elements. Produce, and manufacture from components; ever bitter setback manufactures advantageous components to have "boldness."

1. Boldness to face every life challenge; that "Bold" component is being consistent and firm.

"A person who has doubts is thinking about two different things at the same time and can't make up his mind about anything." *James 1:8 GWV*

2. Boldness to remain resolute. -**having or showing a fixed, firm purpose; determined; resolved; unwavering**.

"But Jesus was matter-of-fact: "Yes—and if you embrace this kingdom life and don't doubt God,

you'll not only do minor feats like I did to the fig tree, but also triumph over huge obstacles. This mountain, for

instance, you'll tell, 'Go jump in the lake,' and it will jump. Absolutely everything, ranging from small to large, as

you make it a part of your believing prayer, gets included as you lay hold of God." *Matthew 21:21 MSGV*

-Robin

How has the chapter provided practical elements and advantageous components to have "boldness"?

Sizakele Mdluli-Chaplin (MBA)

I'm a dynamic international inspirational speaker, author, minister, content creator, and global alopecia advocate and activist. I was born in the beautiful coastal city of Durban, South Africa – now I live with my husband, pastor, in New Jersey, United States.

I'm known as Lady Siza, called to women who have lost their self-worth and self-esteem. My public speaking journey started after she was diagnosed with alopecia. This auto-immune condition mistakenly attacks the hair follicles thus causing the hair to fall out permanently in some cases like her own. I mentor and coach women worldwide by leading, inspiring, and teaching them to be the best they can be and to live their lives with utmost boldness and honesty.

I have degrees in Environmental Health, Public Management, and an MBA. I self-published my first book, "Enough Already"! 'Overcoming the stigmas of Alopecia.' I also co-authored an Amazon bestseller book titled '5 Phenomenal Women'.

Chronicle 5

Get Out

Shonte Youmans

"For the Spirit God gave us does not make us timid, but gives us power, love and self-discipline."
2 Timothy 1:7 NIV

On February 3, 1993, it was a cold and rainy night in Reading, PA. My mom, brother, and I lived at a family member's house because our apartment caught fire. I enjoyed staying at their house because I felt a sense of belonging and love. But little did I know it was slowly coming to an end. My brother and I had just finished eating dinner and heard a voice say, "Go pack up all your clothes."

So we excitedly go pack up our bags, thinking we were moving into a place of our own. Sadly, we were dropped off at yet another shelter; I was devastated. I know we couldn't live with them forever, but at least until my mother found another place and was back on her feet. Ironically she was never back on her feet! Although we found another home, she still didn't take on being a mother; she was still selfish and unwilling to rid her habits. We had a new place, but it was mostly to sleep and take baths, but it was never a home.

My brother and I tried not to stay at the house because it was empty, well, us raising each other. However, our bond became strong, and nothing could come between us, not even the Department of Social Services. We moved into a new place, but life didn't improve; when we were comfortable, a crime was committed in our living room. With both parents being addicts and away from the house, we knew something wrong could happen but never thought a man would be brutally stabbed right in our living room on our sofa! The catastrophe unfolded when my father was arrested for manslaughter and sentenced to eight to ten years.

After all, he had done enough damage to our family with all the mental, physical and emotional abuse he brought into the household. It had been a house full of drunken nights and violence. My brother and I were in the middle of the adult drama. Being taken to bars across the city at all times of the night, no matter the day. There was no apparent regard for their children's academics, physical well-being, emotional well-being, or nutritional efficiency.

I felt so trapped in the chaos that I struggled to find my identity and never used my voice to speak about anything; as a result, people were constantly using me as a footstool. I was the little girl looking for a way to "get out," and little did I know I would get out soon. Don't get me wrong, I loved

Reading, PA, but it weighed on me that I felt like a bu... en to the people that were supposed to love me. Trapped their hurt and never healed, they inflicted their pain on the... children without any knowledge to us. I just wanted t... e a kid and enjoy childhood without being forced to be ... arent.

I was cooking and cleaning a house like a mai... without supervision, and I almost felt obligated to do ... better yet scared of what would happen if I didn't clean or ... ok. It was terrorizing with all the extreme abuse just for bein... alive; I lived in fear of my mother because she made it clea... several occasions that she hated me and couldn't st... d me! I spent a lot of nights crying myself to sleep, wishing I h... another family or why I was even born if no one was ... ing to love me.

I struggled for so long trying to be accepted, th... someday, and finally, my SHERO! I approached her ... asked if I could go back to South Carolina with her. I ... d no idea what it was like to live in South Carolina or the c... ural differences. I was in culture shock and felt a little out ... place simply because it was so rural. I had become accust... ed to walking the streets and accessing stores and restaur... within walking distance. I had to get used to living the... "country life," which took some time.

All I knew was that we needed out, so my brother an... avoided being placed in foster care to live apart. I kr...

going to South Carolina would separate us for a while, but it would not be forever. After a year or so, my brother and I united, but we still had chaos because our mother wasn't mothering. We have an older sister living her best life and not consumed with parenting two younger siblings; the responsibility was too great for a young adult.

Life changed with an opportunity to live with my SHERO and her family. That was pretty cool because she was elated to have me there. My excitement was that someone was showing me love and not a disappointment. I finally felt a sense of relief because "getting out" brought me the love and acceptance I was seeking. Life lesson "getting out" saved our lives.

Get Out Perspective

A bitter setback is a synergetic way to stimulate and facilitate the motivation to develop despite poverty and lack of support. It will provoke you to "get out" by any means necessary.

1. Every trial provokes you to "get out" of every fruitless situation.

2. Every triumph evolves as you transform your spiritual capacity through the Holy Spirit, which gives direction.

-Robin

How has the chapter provoked your perspective on trials and triumph?

_____

_____

_____

_____

_____

_____

_____

_____

Shonte Youmans

I'm a lover of God. A woman whose mission is to impact the world positively. Having faced various challenges life and defied the odds to overcome those circumstances no longer define me. Instead, I've evolved from a broken little girl with no voice, feeling unloved and struggling with her identity, into a woman of substance who strives to be better at womanhood daily.

Throughout life, I've obtained a Bachelor of Arts in Communication at the University of South Carolina-Aiken. Also, I had the opportunity to write and speak about my mess, in which I enjoy sharing my life experiences. In those moments, I realized my mess was my message and a part of my healing. Obtaining a Master of Science in Criminal Justice at Kaplan University was a great challenge, but I completed the task successfully. I'm selflessly loyal by default; I lend a helping hand where necessary. My passion has always been helping others, no matter their capacity. I impact, influence, and intend to be the change to anyone I meet by teaching them, especially women, how to show up as their best selves.

Get in Touch with Shonte

Email: freshstartconsulting20@gmail.com
Instagram: @noteasilyenticed
Tel: 1 (803) 646-2180

Chronicle 6

Unrighteous Judgment

Lady S

"He that is without sin among you, let him first cast a stone at her." John 8:7 KJV

*M*y life existed through titles, theories, and ideologies of others from childhood, well into society's claim of adulthood. I walked, talked, ate, cooked, loved, mothered, worked, controlled investment portfolios, praised, worshiped, and was in wife mode living according to what others stated all my life as to how I should be, for acceptance. Although I was a Pastor's daughter, my life was always in the spotlight. I was to be perfect against all odds. Perfection, according to humankind, is hard to achieve when there are feelings of neglect.

As a child, my only dream was to be an actor and a writer. Unfortunately, my aspiration was short-lived; my parents wouldn't allow me to attend a performing arts school from 1st to 12th grade. It did not fit into their scope of life. While being forced to suppress who I was while attending a school I did not desire to attend, I was molested and introduced to same-sex relationships. That was something I could not bring to my parents. Being put into an adult situation changed my entire outlook on life. To prove that I was not interested in the same sex, I overcompensated with the opposite sex.

My past life consisted of me multiple illicit sexual encounters with different men and minimal women. I had been constantly judged because the spotlight was always on me growing up as the "Pastor' Daughter." They say the Pastor's children are the worse. I lived up to that analogy with no regrets. Since no one was going to look at me past what they saw on the surface to understand why I was doing things that were inappropriate to them, I was going to bandage my hurt and pain with self-soothing. Alcohol, sex, parties, and being a track star of my race. Running from the enemy of low self-esteem, succubus, unnatural affections, ADHD, depression, anxiety, PTSD, bipolar, schizophrenia, masturbation, adultery, molestation, murder, attempted suicide, grief, self-sabotage.

As I ran and became more silent, I was able to zone in on my mother and how with everything that she went through with the good Pastor and her husband, she never complained. Well, not to my knowledge. My father was a caring and loving individual to others outside his house until you crossed him. Then, so often, he's verbally, mentally and emotionally abusive to my mother. Although my father kept my mother in furs, jewelry, and beautiful things, the lifestyle he had to operate to provide materialistic things was unacceptable. When all his family wanted was love.

I looked at my mother as weak; until marriage put me in the same situation. After that, I never wanted to face the problem. I ran from anything that looked, smelled, and reminded me of anything from my childhood. I continuously ran into myself, no matter the street, city, or state where I resided. I ran but could not hide. Although the enemy implanted seeds of destruction, I fostered and nurtured them to grow. In the KJV Version of the Bible, Matthew 7:20 "wherefore by fruits ye shall know them." I ran so much. Pointing fingers at everybody but myself. Until one day, I looked at the rotten fruit around me. I could no longer run from anything because what I was running from was now me.

Too many similarities of past experiences pertaining to my mother arose. However, the abused had become the abuser. My husband's isolation, anger, non-interaction with our children, always defensive, and criticism of my size; I was too skinny for him became toxic. Often made to depend on him, I slowly lost functionality of the right side of my body and could not work. Nothing that I did was right. I reminded him of a past relationship he treated me awful.

I then had the mindset of getting him before he got me. The blows to my face and body never landed, literally. I prepared myself for them, so I abused him with my hands, objects, and statements. I was broken and hurt, but t   t did not matter. I looked good as the trophy wife; no one   ticed the years of pain and torment I carried around. If my   sband looked good, I hit that soprano note; I preached the   of off, constantly doing for others, and I was fine. According   ) others, that is.

My body began to fail; constant pain overtook   e; I couldn't attend engagements nor sing, and I had me   ory loss. Negative statements from people and leaders fr   within the church followed. I was nonsocial, bougie,   arrogant; if I went on, I could draft an entire book on   names and statements alone.

People judged me based on what they saw, n   what they could not see. The same as how I judged my mo   to say, "I will never be like her." Unrighteous judgment c   es when you do not care to know; you watch and run v   what you see. The Bible states in 1 Samuel 16:7, "for the Lor   es not as man sees, for man look on the outward appec   nce, but the Lord looks on the heart. The woman caught i   adultery visibly was caught red-handed. Historically,   law, she could be sentenced to death.

The woman caught in adultery was just like me   ut instead of Yahuah (God) looking at me as people di   e saw my heart. My heart was sinful, and due to the we   t of pain, rejection, disappointment, and neglect, there v   e walls around my heart. It kept me from knowing the difference. So when Yahuah (God) got a hold of me, just like Yeshuah (Jesus) stated to the woman caught in the very act, he told me his prophet, woman, servant, "I don't condemn you, go and sin no more." He saw the matter of my heart.

My deliverance came by me taking the words of Yahuah and choosing to sin no more. It was not easy. Although my mind desired to do right, the evil desires of my body were always present. I realized I was addicted to the lifestyle of sexual divination. I had to take control of it before it took over me again. Having control over one part of my life, I could not understand why I was still angry and lived in fear.

As I continued to work out my soul salvation with fear and trembling, I realized that healing was not there. I had not forgiven myself for allowing people to have control over me. I took hold of my life after an encounter with Yahuah. I had lost my hearing on my right side due to sickness, and Yahuah asked if I wanted to live or die.

I said I am living and doing everything needed. Now my question is how I will complete tasks or take instructions if I cannot hear. Yahuah told me you exist for everyone else and what they desire, forgetting I called you out from among them. I called you into the marketplace. I created you to be in the arena of entertainment to save souls. You will be a light in the darkness.

My life gave me lemons that I have made into's lemonade. I am the author of three books, "From A H o A Housewife," Vol. 1, "My Testimony and Deliverance" V 2. The 3rd book, "Woman," will be released in 2023. A writer, ector, and producer of the full-feature movie "From A Ho to Housewife," to be released in 2023. I have an extensiv acting resume with work to be seen on Hulu and Netflix, with veral stage plays under my belt. I am living the abundant l to die empty to bring Yahuah glory in all that I do by effecti y saving a dying world before Yeshuah Hamashiach re rns when every knee shall bow. Every tongue confesses t he is Lord, and true, righteous judgment takes place.

Critique Perspective

Leading ladies that transformed yield development and evolution through every bitter-sweet season.

Despite others' opinions, you recognize your worth.

1. Your self-worth is the sense of one's value, and worth as a person, self-esteem; self-love and self-respect.

2. Your value is the relative worth, merit, or importance of. The definition of worth is excellence of character or quality as commanding esteem; usefulness or importance, as to the world, to a person, or for a purpose; good or important.

3. Your self-esteem is a realistic respect for or a favorable impression of oneself; self-respect.

-Robin

How has the chapter provided clarity and perspective on reevaluating others' opinions?

_____

_____

_____

_____

_____

_____

Lady S

    I'm a mother of nine children and a grandmother of one—Pastor of Hebrew City located in Philadelphia, Pennsylvania, and Kasumi, Ghana. My apostolic affirmation will be in March of 2023. I was born in December, the last child from the Union of Pastor and Lady of Mount Zion morning Star in South Philadelphia; this is where my ministry, entitled "Women of Deliverance," was founded. Mount Zion is where over 22 years ago, I met my husband while operating as the minister of music; many years later, It's a blessing to be a Pastor alongside my husband—educated in the Philadelphia public, parochial School system. I obtained a medical office assistant certification from Kaplan University in 2009. In 2008, I was ordained an Elder in the Lord's Church. I hold an honorary doctorate in ministry, ordained Bishop in 2018.

    In January 2010, God spoke that the time was now to push out and birth the women's ministry called "Incubated" and write my life story. "For it shall be a movie and on television everywhere for all to see." In October 2010, I hosted "Women Deliverance International," the first annual conference where we served hundreds of women for five days straight, which consisted of prostitutes, exotic dancers, domestic violence victims, single mothers, and much more. Afterward, God spoke to me and said He wanted more of me; now, the book had to come forth.

I wrestled with God unto sickness came upon me causing me to lose all motion ability from head to toe on my right side. One day in March of 2011, I surrendered to God and began to write the book. Within 30 days, the book was complete, then God said to publish it and title it "From a HO to a Housewife" for your life had been inflicted with low decision making. You put yourself in predicaments because of the spirit of succubus, which manifests sexual divination. That sickness was almost to death until I lifted my hand in surrender in the hospital bed at the University of Pennsylvania; within 30 days, a breakthrough happened. My book reached "From a HO to a Housewife" reached International sales in July 2012; the book is now a movie and premiered October 29th, 2022.

Chronicle 7

Never Bitter, Always Better

Michelle Cofer

"Be strong and courageous. Do not be afraid or terrified because of them, for the Lord your God goes with you he will never leave you nor forsake you." Deuteronomy :6 KJV

𝒪ne could find words that lead to someone becoming BITTER; there are just as many words describing what takes to make things BETTER.

Broken	**Bol**...
Insecure	**Eng**...ged
Trauma	**Tec**...able
Tarnished	**Tal**...ed
Excuses	**Effi**...cious
Resistant	**Res**...nt

Often, the only difference between where you are and where you desire to be is a simple shift of perspective. Sadly, as life happens to most people, they tend to focus all their energy on that particular thing going wrong. Instead realizing that, as the Bible says in Job 14:1, "Man that born

70

of a woman is of few days, and full of trouble," many people unrealistically think that life will always be sunshine. When things become bitter, do not focus on that. Instead, focus on the solution. How can something become better?

Will you experience pain? Will you experience setbacks? Will people betray you? Will you experience loss or rejection or feelings of inferiority and insecurity? Absolutely. It's LIFE. But, when life gives you lemons, you should not become BITTER, only BETTER. Look at these two words. They are almost identical, spelled nearly the same, and just as in life, one slight shift in how you view something could change the entire outcome.

In my 44 years, I have had many obstacles that could have made me bitter. As a young child growing up in an environment where drugs or alcohol were a normal part of life, I always wondered; how can I get out of this situation—often bullied because of how I dressed. We were poor on public assistance. I know what it feels like to want more and to fit in. How can I create a life that is better than the one that I currently have?

Romans 8:28, my favorite scripture, has allowed me to look through the lens that says better, even through bitter. Paul reminds us, "For we know that all things work together for the good of them that love the Lord, who are called according to His plan." That is Paul saying; I don't care if life handed you lemons; at some point, you will have to use those lemons to make lemonade.

Imagine being an innocent 6th grader and the person you called "dad" sexually assaults you. Imagine telling your mom, and no one other than her believes you. Yep, it was a turning point for me. On a cold night, I was staying my grandfather's house, and my so-called father, as drunk as he was, climbed into bed with me and my stepmom. I have no idea why he didn't sleep on the sofa or near the far-most side of her. Hours must have passed, and I woke up to him trying to penetrate me.

I kept saying stop. She didn't wake up. He remained on trying, and I would squeeze my legs tighter and tighter to avoid complete contact. Finally, I jumped out of bed and onto the sofa in their room. As soon as it was daybreak I asked my grandfather to take me home. That moment was scary. Life was happening. And as a young girl telling my mom and the doctors and ER staff was frightening; however, because there was no penetration and my hymen was intact, No one believed me. I never saw my "dad" the same.

I began to despise him. I became bitter. Six years later, during a basketball camp, God used me to share the story of resilience that liberated an entire room of teenagers. I discovered my whole basketball team had been molested, raped, or sexually assaulted by a family member or close family friend. That day, at the age of 17-year-old, I began to minister by telling my story. Throughout the years, I would despise seeing him, and then God would touch my heart to do something kind for him. Yes, I could have stayed bitter. Instead, I decided that I owed it to myself and the future to talk about this situation and empower others through it. Now, God enables me to inspire other women to share their truth and never to see themselves as victims but as Victorious.

Here is what I want you to know. The bitterness of lemonade comes from the acidic nature of the lemons, but without the lemon, lemonade cannot exist. Your life may be full of things that don't feel good. You could be facing eviction or dealing with divorce. You may even have lost your income, or even worse, you are grieving the loss of a loved one. No matter what, we know that without those tests, you will never have a testimony. God has encouraged us that people will be overcome by the power of our testimony, so as life become bitter, you focus on what is better. Focus on the promises of God and never lose faith. As a 6th grader, I could have lost hope in God and people because I felt vulnerable and unprotected, but God kept me. When life is squeezing you and times are tough, remember this "it gets better".

Bitter and Better Perspective

Bitter Sweet conditions produce the ability to adapt to many different functions or activities. In addition, "bitter" setbacks enhance your clarity and perspective, making you "better"!

1. Every "bitter" setback reroutes your path to the authentic purpose for existence. "So God created man in His own image, in the image and likeness of God He created him; male and female He created them." *Genesis 1:27 AMPV*

2. Embrace "better" through an affirmed positive posture and embrace your true YAH-given identity. "For we are God's [own] handiwork (His workmanship), [a] recreated in Christ Jesus, [born anew] that we may do those good works which God predestined (planned beforehand) for us [taking paths which He prepared ahead of time], that we should walk in them [living the good life which He prearranged and made ready for us to live]." *Ephesians 2:10 AMPV*

-Robin

How has the chapter provided clarity and perspective on how your "bitter" setbacks made you "better"?

_____

_____

_____

_____

_____

_____

Michelle Cofer

I'm a Kingdom Leader affectionately known as "the PivotHER." I understand the call on my life to help others. Whether doing so from a spiritual place or in the natural realm, I'm passionate about empowering people and impacting change. Through my financial struggles, the girl boss has developed a strong affinity towards helping people overcome the barriers of less-than-excellent credit and financial bondage.

Today, I'm a proud co-owner with my husband Cedric Cofer, of Cofer Financial Group, specializing in Personal & Business Credit, Financial Literacy, Tax Preparation, Business Coaching, & Mentorship. I've penned "365 Affirmed: Prayers for Everyday Living", my first published book. The 2nd book, "PIVOT:101 Ways to Pivot from Bad Credit to Excellent Credit", provides a money mindset tip and practical resource that allowed her to eliminate $54k in debt and build a high credit score.

Understanding that people perish because of a lack of knowledge, I'm committed to traveling nationwide to impact the lives of Millions of Americans with financial challenges. Featured in articles on NBC, CBS, and ABC, listed in BUSINESS

FROM HOME, and celebrated as a top income earner in the network marketing profession. Recognizing I can't reach everyone, I'm committed to impacting as many lives as possible and positioning people to leave a legacy.

Conclusion

This anthology is full of real-life stories, like mine, about women who deliberately decided not to be bitter but better. To view their sour patch moments as an opportunity to peel, cut, boil, and add a little sugar, what was sour became a life-saving pitcher of greatness. At the offset, each reader has received hope to live on, inspiration to forgive, encouragement to love again, and unction to press and pursue your greatness through the arch of life's lemon.

As healing, self-love, self-discovery, and stimulation begin, you may recover your self-esteem, strength, and substance.

"and David inquired of the Lord, "Shall I pursue raiding party? Will I overtake them?" "Pursue them," he answered. "You will certainly overtake them and succeed in the rescue (without fail recover all)." 1 Samuel 30:8 NI

-*Robin*

References

New International Version (NIV)
Holy Bible, New International Version®, NIV® Copyright ©1973, 1978, 1984, 2011 by Biblica, Inc.® Used by permission. All rights reserved worldwide.

The Message (MSGV)
Copyright © 1993, 2002, 2018 by Eugene H. Peterson

Amplified Bible (AMPV)
Copyright © 2015 by The Lockman Foundation, La Habra, CA 90631. All rights reserved.

King James Version (KJV)
Public Domain
In 1604, King James I of England authorized that a new translation of the Bible into English be started. It was finished in 1611, just 85 years after the first translation of the New Testament into English appeared (Tyndale, 1526). The Authorized Version, or King James Version, quickly became the standard for English-speaking Protestants. Its flowing language and prose rhythm has had a profound influence on the literature of the past 400 years. The King James Version present on the Bible Gateway matches the 1987 printing. The KJV is public domain in the United States.

Explore other products!

Apostle Robin

Is known for her unique literature s
powerful enrichment workbooks, a
self-help inspirational books!

Pearls©

- Personal Development
- Women Biblical Charge
- Inspiring Confessions
- Practical Application

$15.99 / Per Book

Side Piece No More©

- Charges women to reject the 2nd position
- Self-Examination
- Positive Affirmations

$12.99 / Per Book

UNMASK ©

- Accountabili   llenge
- Invigorate &   ize
- Practical Sel
- Motivational

$19.99 / P

Contact Now
(980) 349-6140

pastor-robins-website.yola   .com

FEMALE SPEAKER? Platforms AWAITING YOU!

Come take the stage

Apostle Robin

ARE YOU A SPEAKER? JOIN ROBIN ON STAGE AT ONE OF HER FAMOUS WOMEN'S ENRICHMENT OPPORTUNITIES.

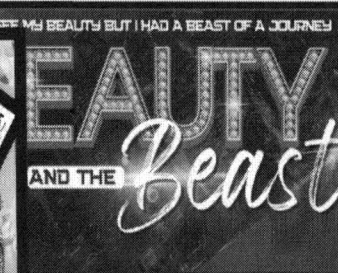

YOU SEE MY BEAUTY BUT I HAD A BEAST OF A JOURNEY

Woman To Woman Impartation

WOMAN TO WOMAN IMPARTATION (WTWI) IS A MINISTRY THAT CELEBRATES WOMEN WITH EXTRAORDINARY STORIES OF VICTORY, TRIUMPH, STEADFASTNESS, BRAVERY, AND GRACE. WTWI TOOK FLIGHT IN FEBRUARY 2013, AFTER A SUCCESSFUL NON-TRADITIONAL IMPACTFUL WAY VIA THE TELECONFERENCE LINE THE ENTIRE MONTH. ALTHOUGH WTWI IS OVERSEEN BY CREATED TO WIN MINISTRIES/APOSTLE ROBIN, IN THE SPIRIT OF EXCELLENCE, WE HOST AN ANNUAL CONFERENCE TO IMPACT WOMEN'S LIVES HOLISTICALLY.

Side Piece No More Workshop

AN ENRICHMENT PROGRAM THAT CHARGES WOMEN TO REJECT THE 2ND POSITION IN ALL REALMS OF LIFE, IN A WORKSHOP SETTING. TOPICS TARGETING BUT NOT INCLUSIVE TO SEXUALITY, SELF-EXAMINATION, INNER HEALING, POSITIVE AFFIRMATIONS, UNVEIL WHY WOMEN PLOT TO DESTROY OTHER WOMEN, AND REINFORCEMENTS TO TACKLE SELF-SABOTAGE AND SELF-HATRED!

Beauty and the Beast Workshop

AN ENRICHMENT PROGRAM THAT ENCOURAGES WOMEN TO EMBRACE THEIR UNIQUENESS AND BEAUTY. THE OUTER BEAUTY DID NOT STOP THE BEAST OF THEIR JOURNEY HOWEVER THIS WORKSHOP ENLIGHTENS THEM HOW STRENGTH CAN BE FORTIFIED. THE BEAST OF FEAR, DEPRESSION, FAILURE, TRAUMA, ABUSE, ABANDONMENT, REJECTION, ADDICTIONS, BETRAYAL, AND LOSS IS NOT THE END OF THE STORY. WOMEN CAN STRATEGICALLY ALIGN SUCCESSFULLY, STAND, AND BE VICTORIOUS NOW WITH A BEAST-TESTIMONY!

Contact Now
(980) 349-6140

pastor-robins-website.yolasite.com

Made in the USA
Columbia, SC
15 November 2023